FORGIVE ME IF NONE OF THIS IS TRUE

Poems

ILENE STARGER

Also by Ilene Starger

Lethe, Postponed

FORGIVE ME IF NONE OF THIS IS TRUE

For further information, or with correspondence,
please contact Ilene Starger:

istarger@earthlink.net
c/o P.O. Box 246
FDR Station
New York, NY 10150

Cover Photograph by Pedro J. Pérez
Used with kind permission

Author Photograph © Lois Greenfield
Used with kind permission

Cover design and typesetting by Odyssey Books

First Edition 2014
Rara Avis Books
New York
Printed in the United States of America

Library of Congress Control Number: 2014953567

ISBN 978-0692307991

ACKNOWLEDGMENTS

The author gratefully acknowledges the publications listed below, in which the following poems first appeared:

Plunge — *Manzanita*
Summer — *Grasslimb*
Beyond the Fourth of July — *Grasslimb*
Two Thanksgivings — *Oyez Review*
Equilibrium — *SecondWind*
Toward Positano — *Folio*
For Medea, Waking — *Oberon*
Epitaph — *Bayou*
After Icarus — *Paper Street*
As With Emma Bovary — *Tributaries*
Believing Venice — *Oberon*
Drought — *TarWolf Review*
Pilgrimage — *Poesia*
Rue de Varenne — *Bayou*

The poems comprising the *Lethe, Postponed* section in this volume were published in chapbook form by *Finishing Line Press* as Lethe, Postponed © 2008 by Ilene Starger

Special thanks to Leah Maines and Kevin Maines of *Finishing Line Press* for their kind and enthusiastic support.

Gratitude to Tracy K. Smith and Jacob Miller, who shared their knowledge and offered encouragement during the making of many poems in this collection.

Thank you to the teachers and writers who enrich one's life and quietly alter the world.

For my mother and father,
who might understand

(I wish that I could warm my hands
and sit with you awhile)

Foreword by the Author

In a cacophonous world, does poetry still matter?
Perhaps the times we live in are no more turbulent
than those which preceded us.

Words and silence are what we have.

Poets report, invent, prefer not to explain.
We fret about the sequencing of poems; we hope
to string together a story of sorts which might speak to you.

Your eye finds a page in a book;
you conjure up the story.

Ilene Starger

DECEMBER 31, 11:59 P.M.

Clearing of the throat; shiver; expectation.
Practiced eyes dilate with what-will-be:
yearning, champagne-induced. Wordless
invitation as life, finite parcel, drops
itself down. Love-soaked, love-deprived,
choice hovers like a downpour
which can't make up its mind.
Possibility, disco-ball bright, commingles
with the body's trespasses, willed; blind.
Numerous invitations.
Stillness before changeover.
Thinking that, if one looks hard
enough, one can detect new air
settling in for the year.

FORGIVE ME IF NONE OF THIS IS TRUE

Poems

ILENE STARGER

Rara Avis Books

TABLE OF CONTENTS

Pilgrimages

LAST RITES

And green. And bloom, turning to clouds.
Did they, clouds, notify you that years
would be returned, opened, slightly used;
soiled? Numerous lives you have lived,
shrugged off, but the thing of it is,
you haven't buried them, not as yet.
Green blossoms taunt you. Night sweats
soak your garments straight to the skin:
black garments, torn with mourning.
The stroke of a heavy clock:
a lover's eyelash on your cheek.
Now, what do you wish to tell us?

VILLAGE

Just beyond the hill
there are horses.
They drink from a stream

cooler than human
imagining; they bend
in the shadow of a steeple;

bow their heads
in private prayer,
color of evening.

Daylight, premature,
will jostle quiet creatures
into locomotion;

carriages will overflow
with passengers, unseeing.
Their guardians –

horses, stoic, gleaming –
must guide them over
unmarked roads.

All the rutted sorrows,
left unspoken
by those who ride here.

BEGINNING

You were certain of things – no peace in this lifetime;
people, unchanging; your need to be alone;
my hair leading your hand on
as it brushed my neck, warm against
your chest of taut beliefs. Our first May night
masqueraded as August: drunken sky, wet
and stiff, too many clothes, inadequate
intervals of breath. I hoped you'd stop
talking and kiss me where I wanted
to be kissed. Spurned by silence,
I pinned myself to your sleeve;
wondered if you were right
about my wanton hair, the state
of the world, your unromantic soul.

BELIEVING VENICE

We've awakened here, those summers
when flirtatious green-gray water
seduced us, through *finestras* framed by heavy shutters
opened out on day. Now we've come in winter,
chilled by sudden changes in our nocturnal weather.
The *motoscafo*'s rude spray slap offends my tender
cheek; disoriented, we touch on land, and with our
heavy baggage, seek out antique splendor.
We'll collect churches and *Tintorettos*; I'll render
you – pale, churlish – through my camera lens.
At the *soffiatura del vetro*, I'm rapt, yet mindful of a cinder
floating near my jealous eye. When night, opaque, descends,
my mouth on you will make a shape: outsized, soon to shatter.
Tomorrow: *dolci*, souvenirs; none of this will matter.

IMAGINING ENCELADUS

Saturn, embarrassment of riches:
moons aplenty, ripe, for lovers,
their midnight embraces.
To choose, forsake, define

in a moment's hesitation;
heaven help us
with our plummeting.
Why shouldn't Saturn

keep Enceladus to itself?
Fourth-largest moon,
fourth favorite child.
Dreams, out of sequence,

shuffled like poker cards;
emblazoned with silver-toned light.
We lift our eyes
heavenward,

and, in our embarrassment,
make excuses
for ourselves as we crouch
toward God.

Enceladus, moon
of ice crystals,
of psychedelic colors:
now that's the place to be.

EVEREST

When being desired by you was reason
and folly; when there was nothing
but the prize – crystalline, vertiginous –
of you beckoning, I pushed on toward
one summit in willful ignorance
of my lack of readiness and right equipment:
lungs small, petulant; legs yearning
for reprieve; pickaxe left behind; ropes
I carried flimsy, unreliable, almost human.
What I'd have after victory, I couldn't name;
I hadn't counted on time's
chilly descent. White fatigue, so familiar,
as my body's expectant blankness
merged with snow: the snow and I kept vigil for
your stealthy marking of territory, silent theft.
Yet some transactions, once completed, lay claim
to dissolution into thin air – *tenuem auram* –
when one has climbed far from sight.

AUBADE

See, it's all right:
so much dark blue breaking
and entering
where it has no business being.
Be grateful nonetheless.
A cacophony of clocks,
their poorly kept secrets:
minutes conspire
with eternity, but look,
it's all right.
A symphony of stars late
for morning prayers,
when just one prayer will do:
"More love awaits,
of that we are certain."
One dark blue fragment –
special delivery –
insists on gaining entry.
Clocks, stars pay homage
to what has gone;
what continues.
Already, dimmed specks
poised in the late sky –
a pointillist's vision –
unpack instruments
for their concert
this evening.

NARROWING

You walk/feel your way along a corridor
of thinning poplars:
they mirror your thinning hair
and thinning chances.
You bless the Lord for this subtle reminder,
subtraction of what you've done
from what you were originally given.

In this modest forest,
you are dwarfed
by nature's taunts, testament
to lasting things.
Winter's brisk mistakes,
brief lament undone
by unvarnished truth.

Walking/feeling your way along a corridor
of splendid poplars,
you vow to discard the self-help pages,
the hashish pipes,
hallucinations of glory.
Under the influence,
winter evaporates;

it is not a given
that other seasons will follow.
Traffic lanes,
dotted with white, constrict.
Soon, your days will be pencil-thin.
Wisps of smoke,
proof of winter's breath,

will be hard to spot,
even if the corridor
of thinning poplars
has, in its midst, clean,
unobstructed spaces
for your viewing pleasure.

LEAVING THE ORPHANAGE

Morning glints off a metal bed, where
his fingers gently trace his skin;
proof of self, warmth found there,
since daily bread, scant
comfort, rests in a stranger's hand.
Perhaps this Sunday he'll be chosen:
his shirt is starched; heart, well-hid;
its homely beat refuses to be chastened.
Shy introductions; careful, cadenced
laughter of those who would claim him.
As they leaf through his condensed
childhood, bundled belongings slip loose:
uncertainty, shame, gratitude
mingle with the solace born of solitude.

EXILE

Shuttered room
no man's land
of your own making
religious doubt
beckons
tempting basilisk
parameters of loss
pulsing light
meager compensation
when wishing for
the migraine-bright
stab of stars

Spoiled masochist
you turn cruel
when your failures
tip the scales
the next hour
crackles bright
sliver of redemption
until shutters
foreclose on
your comfort zone
declaring it
off-limits

ON FAITH

The phone call came
at first I could not tell if you were laughing
or keening like Belfast fathers
who kneel over bloodstained sons
they never had a prayer
in a world which unmoors the firmest of men

The call came
you witnessed words which altered time
bent light brought you reeling to the floor
stole the safe deposit box stashed in your soul
all at once your sanctity was soiled
so you railed at the oblivious day

I cloak my sins in holy dust
seek comfort in your body
it has taught me things namely

The heart is a sacred burial ground
it can be blasphemed
it cannot be paved over

As a boy
you believed birthdays
would last forever like the moon
you hoped to lasso
and possess
pristine love not yet invented

Oh I've tried
to warn you
there are limits and they hurt

QUESTIONS FOR THE DALAI LAMA, GOD, THE UNIVERSE, GANESHA, BUDDHA AND THE MAN ON THE CORNER OF EAST 60TH STREET

Dressed in your tiny, dark-quilted parka,
you sit, most mornings,
on a prosperous sidewalk
in a neighborhood where the best shoes and handbags are sold.

You have no legs; only chubby stumps for arms.
An ageless soothsayer
clutching a worn paper cup, you are mostly head and torso.
Uncommon light – part halo, part store window reflection –
surrounds you.

Although you used to frighten me, I find you quite beautiful.
Don't think me racist,
but your skin is glossy, rich: the color of hot chocolate
at Angelina's in Paris.
Maybe we could go there, together.

I'd like to ask how it happened, but I'm too polite.
(Was it Thalidomide? Viet Nam? A crushed automobile?)
Was there no mother
to feed you apples and pudding,
then brush her hair against your cheek?

Was it a cruel quirk of fate, ridiculous,
like children chained to metal beds in distant countries,
or abandoned, starving, on our streets?
Nearby babies, left in high school bathroom garbage cans
on prom night.

Who could smell a baby's skin and trash the memory?

I've imbued you with magical powers.
Does the moon drop you down to this same spot before dawn?
Do you go home to anyone?
Who cleans your filth? Do you rage at the ceiling,
or use it for dreams?

I could be your Dorothy; you, my Scarecrow.
You could move in with me:
I'd roast you a chicken with forty cloves
of garlic, or forty pieces of gold, whichever you prefer.

We could share the details of each day;

discuss Botticelli; Mozart; string theory.
Do you know about Lucy and Ethel
stealing John Wayne's footprints
from Grauman's Chinese Theatre,

or the perfect June tomato, eaten with feta on a black pebble
Santorini beach?

A lover's mouth, generous, forbidden?

For the price of a bagel and a cup of coffee,
maybe you could explain
why, with more gray hairs marring the mirror every morning,
I still think of myself as an orphan.

We're not that different, so could you touch the hem
of my camel hair coat and bless me?

I don't want to know how many years I've been given:
that's too greedy, or finite.
I'd settle for a guarantee of love, sudden
arrival, green bird on the windowsill.

The world tilts: Tower of Pisa; the Cyclone ride at Coney Island;
my view of things, at times.
I'd be fine if another's lips could warm my neck; if his hands
could heat the breakfast toast.

Answers, please:
if I make my bed each day; floss;
pen thank-you notes in delicate calligraphy;
clear the bathtub drain;
radiate kindness to one and all,
will night blanket me?
Will I ascend? Will Rhett Butler swirl me in his cape?
Could a miniature soul – wet, wrinkled – find succor in my body,

or have decades of menstrual blood been prelude without coda?

I'm afraid of earthquakes.
I'm afraid of words forsaking me.
I fear a long, narrow life; I'd choose one that's brief,
but illuminated.

Until clouds occlude us,
I will pray to you: my oracle,
false idol,
magnificent leper.

I will embrace you, declare you whole,
if you will do the same for me.

HOURGLASS

Destiny's marker, in its elusive form:
a roiling ocean, dark vat of hope;
more turbulent than Lourdes,
that delicate medicine for those
who, balm-deprived,

cleanse themselves of procrastination
by virtue of religious droplets.
An ocean, unjust, reads its roll call.
Supplicants kneel, *carpe diem*
stamped tardily on their foreheads.

CARTOGRAPHY

In dreams, I am courted
by cobalt seas, pearls strung
on leaves, time collapsing
in on itself. Each kiss spans
centuries, or seconds.

In the post, a letter, prescient;
pinned to an ancient map.
Confident, elegant,
your winged calligraphy
seduces me.

Becalmed in love's waters,
I survey your island.
Like Columbus, you're triumphant:
deft explorer of my flesh, or
your own uncharted restlessness?

A dream, mere blueprint for happiness.
Set sail with this; return to this.

FLIGHT

He excretes the private grief of men:
salt, iron, sulfur, body's swift betrayal.
His sentry heart has failed to guard
against what hardens him: gardenia-ed
women everywhere, mouths to drink
from, silks unraveling, like memory

He forgets the choosing of a life:
soul conjoined with mouths to feed,
mortgages, the rented dream,
tuxedo, dentist's chair; the right fork
for the salad plate, the swearing off of alcohol,
at least on homework nights. He conjures
up his wife, before babies, change of life:
avid breasts, open mind; now, she's thickened,
unmoved by his tongue;
immune to him, like those girls from Catholic school,
converts to virginity, its close-mouthed kiss
best left in the dark.
He labors for this life: time card to keep,
the drilling down of broken streets;
or stringing words to light a poem, sonnet
spent on silver things, which can't be
fully grasped. Women he will never know,
shiny in their cellophane; he walks
his fingers down their backs,
where wings are formed, and sins absolved,
as days stretch out in luxury,
no debt or doubt to stop the watch

or choke the serene garden.
He sits across from her: cozy mealtime pal,
mother of his progeny,
keeper of his cock, and laundry list;
scholar of his schoolboy games, soldier schemes;
of the tiny astronaut he was,
ablaze with grown-up glory,

escaping then from earthly weight;
countdown, all the ticking sounds:
rapid clock, rapacious heart

TEMPTATION

Where, first, it forms: on the tongue, dark
realm; a word, your birthright,
uttered in rapturous contemplation
of the object desired. Rain –
preternatural, gleaming –
was promised, but crawl
toward light, the fickle kind;
keep it close, like religion.
Claim, for your own, obsidian
eyes: flaws intact, alluring.
Unveil your harlot-shaped mouth
as you recline –
bathed, perfumed, sacrificial –
on love's pyre, center of life; its blood.

PILGRIMAGE

Don't make me unlearn you.
Lend me your *y* chromosome,
if only to study the weight, in grams,
of your breath on my torso.
I altered a word in a poem, for you.
I wouldn't do that for just *anybody.*
You've made a sham of my pride.
Peculiar quiet of a hit-and-run scene:
I'm lonesome tonight.
Did you mean what you said
about searching for Bethlehem?
Your masculine tendencies:
you murmur something about holiness
while inhaling my scent.

CIRCUS

They drive from town to town
in caravans; the trucks are magic-
filled. The bearded lady, the fire-
eating man, the saddest clown
you'll ever see, all here for
your amusement. Most people like
the circus. Are you perceptive?
Do you look behind the tent flap?
Tell us what you see: seediness,
the flattened side of human nature?
Or flame, pageantry? Red-gold
splendor behind the eye,
as when you tumble into a wondrous
sleep, and it's all in your head,
your own movie. You are young,
daring; you hardly recognize
yourself, all feathers and spangles.
You are nine years old. You fly.
Your fate will not be as you imagine
it; no tent could contain
such immensity. But you don't glean
this. You dream. You are sticky
with treats and youth. Hypnotized
by sawdust, a trapeze,
your own gaudy desire,
you swear you'll join the circus.

PALACES

One by one, the movie houses of my youth
vanish; already this year, several
have fallen under the wrecking ball's
spell. Before multiplexes, dreams:
I prefer mine rendered in silver.
I dislike gaudy color, noise; yet was born
too late for Valentino and his ilk.

One adolescent summer, when
I would do anything for boys, and
to evade heat's grip, I sought out the air-
conditioned pleasures of Manhattan's
movie theaters, a different one each week.
Each week, virginity lost. Thursday
afternoon: a plush, high seat. I looked

good in my jeans and red halter top.
I settled in, let the film wash over me
like July. From the seat behind,
a man's hand — unknown — gently brushed
my cool shoulder, my sun-streaked back.
Curious, shivering, aroused, I turned
to stare; turned, again, to focus on the screen.

So this was life.

DROUGHT

No one tells you that tears, like eggs,
are to be bartered, or that their supply
is finite: they will, like your blood,
diminish to a fine, thinning trickle.
As years pass, this legacy of *larmes*
seems pitifully meager. Youthful,
you had rivers at your disposal;
as a yearning adolescent, unsure
of what the body was meant for, tears,
perverse comfort, were your inevitable
companions. It's not that hurting
stops, or promiscuous ducts go dry;
perhaps grief, conspicuous,
fails to impress the yawning day.

POEM FOR EMMETT TILL'S MOTHER

Your son was just a boy, fourteen years of age;
his only crime: the color of his skin.
I was not yet born in 1955;
I would come into the world soon enough
to witness what we had wrought in Mississippi.

Your son wore a hat and tie;
he was a city boy, Chicago-born.
I'm sure you taught him well; in photographs,
his smile and fawn-like eyes
make me feel ashamed of the color of my skin.

Your son whistled — so we said —
at a woman who was white;
at night, we dragged him from his bed;
beat his body down; shot him full of holes;
dumped him, blind, into the Tallahatchie River.

Such whistling by Emmett on the wind:
elusive, sweet; a pure-toned sound.
His adolescent quest for love, brave mischief,
was quite innocent; would have gone unnoticed
but for the color of his skin.

I might place a wreath over your son's heart;
I might lament our cowardice,
corroded sense of justice; our empathy
abducted by the world
into which we have been born.

If I could feel your breath on my wrong-colored skin,
I might say I know your boy
smiling out at me from newspapers, magazines:
the way he looked, your boy,
before our world interfered.

We said he whistled at a woman.
He was addressing heaven.

HERA'S LAMENT

In a *taverna* across time,
Hera's eyes flash fire at Zeus.
She loves him with such force.
The sheer weight
of her passion continues
to astonish her. She is done.
She thinks she is done.
Passion exhausts her.
The couple drinks clouded wine.
They argue over details: when
and how Aphrodite came
between them.
Plates get broken; blame
is assigned; fury,

flung across the room.
With desire's shifting allegiances,
its aftershocks, the *taverna's*
tables tremble. Zeus knows
better than to argue
with woman or goddess.
Hera believes that men,
even gods, are cruelly weak.
The ground undulates;
roars with acrimony.
What seemed solid shifts
under Hera's feet. The *weight*,
she thinks, *love's weight*: it
takes its toll on a body.

OUT OF PIRAEUS

You gave me the sea –
you fastened sapphires, stained
with the Aegean, to my wrist;
a bashful sailor, you'd trawled
shops along the square for
Aphrodite's treasure, hidden deep
in your shirt pocket. Hope's
spray – beribboned, salty promise –
leapt from smog-shrouded city
stones; was heralded by
impertinent auto horns.
Ancient temples chaste
with scaffolding envied us,
new lovers, clad in waves.

ON HOLIDAY

Paris. A hotel courtyard framed
by emerald leaves: elegant birds hum
jazzy notes while awaiting their supper.
Can this miniature Eden shade us?

Wednesday, we'll visit cathedrals;
marvel at saints who shunned pleasure
for sacrifice. I choose the former:
fromage blanc; lilac-scented bathwater;

your naughty, practiced hands.

Tonight, we'll put on our finery;
go to the opera, where life sounds
better sung than spoken. With music
behind us, I'll ask for the moon. Smile,

say nothing, just whirl me along any
cobblestone street; give me pleasure, like
the *framboises* we shared in that empty café.
Its owner kissed both of my cheeks

and saw someone else in my eyes.

ROUSSEAU'S DREAM

Follow your itch. Down a Congo-dark alley
you'll walk, as muddy gravel crunches underfoot.
Smashed figs and silver remnants of rum bottles
remind you that you are now in a country
where, from time to time, you'll need to pull
your sheepish passport photo from its hiding place.

You could start over here. You could be new.
You could blend with men in sweat-soaked undershirts
fragrant with cologne and motor oil.
At the end of the day, these men cook goat stew and
dance to whatever jive sounds the local radio station sends
them. Emptied out, they sleep in ragged states of grace.

Follow me. Tonight, there is only this to consider:
A leaky moon. Fingers, curled around duty-free love.
Urgent, wordless promises.
My hibiscus scent on your fugitive skin.
Lie back.
Eyes closed. You can trust me.

BEWARE OF SHINING THINGS WHICH LIE ON THE GROUND

A princess, riding in a carriage
near a parapet erected by soldiers
occupying the town,
notices an object – tiny, glittering –
half-embedded in the ashen ground of winter:
object of desire or danger?
The princess asks her coachman
to investigate; he steps down
from the carriage, and scoops up
the small, glittering sphere. He brings
it to her for closer inspection.
If this were a fairytale, the coachman
would hand a diamond to the princess,
would deposit it, for safe-keeping,
into her dainty, gloved, hand.
But this is not a fairytale; the found
object is not a diamond. It is a fragment
of war. It is a twisted bit of the future,
cold and ashen as winter. The princess,
protected by velvet cloaks and furs,
cannot make out what the glittering object is.
The coachman, illiterate, does not
have the proper word for it.
Certain that it is no treasure, the princess
throws it back on the frozen ground,
where, in fifty years or so,
it will sprout into a scarred, violent shrub,
blotting out what paltry beauty
remains of the landscape.

CLASS SYSTEM

At bleary, beginner's dawn
(hung-over workday), a brace –
gaggle (or is that term reserved for geese?) –
of pigeons scampers for crusts
of bread on a filthy sidewalk.
Alone, noticeably apart
from them, one pigeon,
white of plumage,
topaz-eyed, bestows his majesty
upon this run-down neighborhood.
Observing him, I think (don't know why)
"White Russian."
He seems descended from a throne,
of regal bird ancestry;
he looks to me as if he could recite poetry,
a bit of Brodsky, perhaps, or Mandelstam
(laborers, both; revered, suppressed at home.)
The other pigeons fight for bread;
one, proud, waits to be served.
I'd confide that I'm a poet,
but (in the company of those he's read)
I'm a lowly servant,
unseen by them,
and this noble bird.

SWIMMING THE DESERT

Amphibious, I prefer ocean to dry rock;
indistinct wetness to truth's prick,
courtesy of cacti. I must remain vigilant.
Still, there is grace:
a late sky, bowed with grief's
purple shadings. Afternoon, the scorch
of passionate arms, deceptive safety.
"Don't forget," I tell myself,
"heatstroke can kill." Love's dream, hatless,
recumbent in the sun: such light,
unchecked, will wither us. I crawl away.

Superstitious, I search Indian trails
for talismans to ward off life, the blistering.
Nature, nurturing villainess:
"Don't forget," I tell myself, "its bounty
sears the eye." Harsh evanescence.
No waves of sand here,
just parched opportunity. Sooner
or later, the past catches up: its headline
informs me that I – random, dry –
am disappearing. God, crafty,
has begun my submergence.

RUE DE VARENNE

Ma chère Camille —

The fire has given out. Night
cuts through my coat and vest,
the layers of *mes vêtements*,
the layers of my heart.
There is hunger in my belly,
not just for wine and bread.

There are many kinds of hunger:
for your skin, cool, veined like marble;
for silken stone which succumbs to my will;
for torsos, hair and braided limbs
where none before existed.
I grope for *Les Trois Ombres*;

I greet the day with thoughts of you.
You are not beside me; your scent
remains. Rained-on linen sheets
cannot soothe my fever.
I fear I've done too little;
I fear I've done enough.

Ecstasy unleashed wears chains,
chien sauvage qu'il faut dompter.
If I could outsmart this faint hope
which keeps me in place and alert,
I'd forge truth with my mind, not bare
hands, and sculpt fresh forms in dreams.

My naked hands, so far from yours,

hoard time, and hold the future
as it breaks apart.
The fire has gone out. The furnace,
weak, is reluctant to finish
its work of branding my soul with stars.

By day, desire and iron mingle
to birth the fine-boned faces of our art.
By night, I face *La Porte de l'Enfer*:
no glassine moon,
no glance from you,
no molten kiss to stoke this ashen heart.

Toujours,
A. Rodin

39

SPLIT

Yours no longer, I lose track of streets:
on errands, the commonplace seems
strange, unmapped. In the midst of cellphone
signals, I speak to no one. A thousand
blood-orange suns have perished since
we first met: delicacy, smashed
by brutal silence. We are capable
of unspeakable things. I am wrong,

divided, congratulating the self
which admits you are a charlatan;
loathing the self prostrate on the altar
of your papier-mâché soul. Countless
cellphone signals transmit loss;
weep for our demise.

TRAINS

Behind the madness of thought,
there is language.
"If you can dream it, you can do it," boasts
an advertisement for a gadget
that we do not need.
The speed of light. Six million gone.
Absence inscribed on frozen earth.
The shorn hair, pounds of it. Gold, spelled
like God, but with an 'l,' and diamonds,
plucked from frozen fingers:
the wedding bands. Braids of prayer,
the challah breads;
kaddish in the synagogues, burnt words
on the lips at Shabbat dinners
in the towns
where they were plucked, from their beds;
from the dignity of nothing much to take with them.
Not my kin, these people who resembled me.
And I lapse into tiny prayers.
The skein of human suffering.
And I, a Jewess, wait, in Times Square, for trains.
Just as they did; well, no, *they* are *me*;
six million names, shower
of linguistics in the summer heat;
their names on battered leather
cases which they clutched,
new word for *fear*,
as they stood; the wait for trains,
in frozen heat. Trains to destinations read

41

aloud by me: *Treblinka. Majdanek. Mauthausen.*
Theresienstadt. Belzec. Sobibor. Auschwitz-Birkenau.
And so. On and on, the foreign sounds,
linguistic fury for the ears, terror
in each lilting syllable.
On the train today, a woman praised her co-worker.
"He's very nice, for a Jew," she said.
I could neither stare, nor look in another direction.
I could have appealed to the other passengers.
An appeal to reason.
My destination is not known to me. I am a Jewess.
I've kept my hair; I keep it long;
it may not keep for long. I've lost a tooth;
I've lost my love. Each night, I remind myself of this,
as I remove the diamond band
from my tender finger;
not the wedding one, but still, one dear to me.
One I need, like blood; like God, gold without the 'l.'
I am reminded when I come in at night.
Last night, the floor
above me shook with love:
midnight cries of sex, quite tiresome
as I tossed, celibate, in a turned-down bed.
Temporary solution to the frozen heat of love.
If you can dream it, you can do it.
They – not my kin – dreamed it, and *they* did it.
Blueprinted it, in fact. Most evidence destroyed,
but some remains. I look away.
I shut my ears.
And wait for trains,
in Times Square, in wintertime.

My clothes are warm. I burn, with cold; with missing them,
six million war-torn,
warm, from familiar beds.
We must not turn away.
"So love your life,' I tell myself, 'Love its grievous imperfection."
The missing bits, the overflow, the nights
that are like water
dripping on the roof, while sex goes on above,
noisy benediction.
"Love this life," I tell myself, "Love its daily pile of unpaid bills."
The graveyard that one visits yearly,
the bakery that one shouldn't visit every day,
but one does, in search of something sweet
like early-hour conversation.
We must love the sound of trains, harsh and evanescent.
Beyond the madness, there is what remains.
Six million gone.

Lethe, Postponed

ABSENCE

The year without you began: quaint
ordinariness. One jam jar, sweet
with daisies, graced our kitchen table;
October's colors clung to walls.
Beyond a cool expanse of hallway,
your bicycle stood patiently in wait
for this amnesiac's journey: swift
denial of your smell, feel; slow
and lethal grin, unerring in its aim.

Exalted, you could have held still.
What pure exhalation had I
witnessed, finished breath falling
from your body, or my own?

PLUNGE

Risk-averse, contrary, we entrust
ourselves to whitewater; as day goes
down along these banks, courage leaks
from the soles of our rubber shoes
made for gripping bottom, careless
stopping place. On the Tuolumne, each
low-hanging branch seems close enough
to touch if the current gets complacent. Details
in the distance, gauzily familiar, remind us
that we mourn summer's ragged grass; candles,
sparse, atop crooked chocolate cakes;
love, close enough to touch, fathomless.
Fire, river, air: tricky symbols, unforgiving,
like the years which weight this raft.

OFF THE FARM

The cows went first.
Knowing that something had
gone terribly wrong with the world,
they packed up their trunks
for travel and set out to warn
the other animals. They exited cinder-strewn

pastures and silos gray with foreboding.
The barns could no longer contain
their bodies. Something in the world
had gone awry, and cows knew
they must sound the bell of reason,
of actions and such consequences.

The cows gathered up family photos,
and warm cloaks for winter, oncoming.
The cows would provide their own food.
They had the need for music, and
memorized simple melodies
for moonlight serenading when darkness,

leaden and un-soulful, would make it tough
to breathe. The cows were first to go.
Not sure how to tell the others
that the world was finishing,
they conferred among themselves
as stars, unpaid, shut down.

TROMPE-L'OEIL

Before charcoal evening erases itself;
before florid promises stain my lips;
before the magnifying lens
of familiarity shrinks
our mythic souls;
before your objections burrow
into my obedient body (burning,
idyllic only in darkness);
before we unravel
borrowed spiderwebs of sleep
and disembark this slippery ship;
before we remember
if time hurtles toward us
or stands still;
before dawn scatters
opalescent marbles
across the floor,
disregard my stubborn longing:
a frescoed backdrop,
exposed as fraudulent
if struck by direct sunlight.

KNOWLEDGE

His arrival at the middle point
of his time on Earth
has startled him into an assessment
of what he does
and does not understand.

The status quo: pavement split,
bloody with broken roses,
color of a beggar's
regurgitated breakfast.
Each step he takes confirms

the gap between himself, fragile,

and the inverse of fear.
Being afraid, he cannot peer
into love's guts,
pomegranate-sticky.

His arrival at the point
of compromise: his knees buckle.
He contemplates the latter
half of life *sans* illusion,
torn safety net.

He takes into consideration
youth's arrogance,

its cool smile;
the arranging of the world
according to whim, and hunger.

He puts on his reading glasses;
reaches for a dictionary,
atlas, book of etiquette.
He would like an explanation,
or at least an apology.

FERRIS WHEEL, 1966
(for J.S.)

Dormant by day, a steel colossus;
at night, high-powered neon, glorious.
I begged you to take me to it,
centerpiece of the country fair;
August sign of summer's passing.
Much unsaid beneath bright surfaces.
I begged you to lead me to it,
paradise, found: the Wheel,
pleasure palace, rentable
for one dollar.

Coupled behind the safety bar,
we sat in our private car, an awkward
father-daughter pair.
Urged on by electricity and shouts,
the Wheel, ringed planet,
began its rotation. We rose
above our lives; gravity was gone.
Your sweater hugged my shoulders.
Suspended, we seemed close
to stars; we dipped into their silence.

You would leave us soon.

I saw it in the distance, asterisked,
the price of flood-lit beauty.

The Wheel's gears, jittery, groaned;
descent, toward slow ground.
We grew dizzy with the ending:
our dollar's worth, one ride.

Another century; starred
words, suspended, in cool dark.

LETHE, POSTPONED

Late, for crying out; night's
tear-damp face can't comfort
you, nor furtive glances
at the door: high, impregnable.
Mother's love lies
down the hall, faintly lit
by yawning fire; impervious
to need (weak, thirsty,
nearly tall.) Surrender, then
to shadowed sleep; see
specters dance across a wall:
they might have risen,
differently, in another house;
in a tranquil dream.

SUMMER

There is silent understanding
between them: the small girl who waits
patiently on a bench
outside a shop, and the pug chained
to a lamppost near the bench.
Each day, the girl tallies up her losses.
She waits for them, expected guests.
The pug does not like his chains;
his grasp of freedom strains his leash.
The girl and the pug, abandoned, perspire.
Each leave-taking may be brief;
ice cream and a park may be in the offing.
Death (small, clever) disguises itself.

ARTIFACT

While gathering items for the storage bin,
I excavate the book,
buried beneath winter's woolen pile
of scarves, sweaters, gloves.
We are dormant.
Now it's June:
snowflakes seem impossible,
a child's fantasy, tucked tight
inside a manufactured globe.
A leftover Christmas gift,
resplendent in red tissue paper,
the book was meant for you.
Not quite forgotten,
decked out in passion's obvious color,
it has awaited your return.
When we were like children,
these things seemed possible:
snowflakes; truth in togetherness;
giving up the ghost
of the past, its failures.
Unaware that you'd silently cut loose
from *us*, what *we* meant,
I bought you a gift:
a book of poems
whose title held special meaning.
Months chased the wind;
the book slept, in case you cared
to reconsider.

It's June now:
winter must be put to bed.
A book, parcel of hope, ghost
of Christmas past.
I'll just tear off the tissue paper;
give myself a gift.

CHAIR

What has prompted it to turn
against you, after years of affectionate
embracing? The bump in the dark, unseen
obstacle, friend no longer; your shin,
foolish, bruised like the heart. Knobby
collision of bone, wood and nail, encouraged
by your spiteful flesh, its oath of loyalty
scorned by time. Objects of comfort renege
on their promises: bargains made shabby
by years of neglect and blind faith.

BEYOND THE FOURTH OF JULY

You're stretched out in summer's *longueur*;
the light, divine sorcerer,
plays all kinds of tricks.
There is this paradox:
your life contracts
with each day's waltz around the sun.
The days — white and black
like dominoes;
or sometimes silver-tipped;
each a pleated accordion —
fall in on themselves
trying to please you.
There are moments:
haze lifts; hot pink light,
all firecracker-ed music,
enters and expands your soul.
The specific jingle
of the ice cream truck;
stolen ghetto blaster funk;
song of a pampered nightingale,
no matter: everything melts,
despite the deception
of slow-moving days.
Your life contracts.
Still, it's summertime.

THE WEIGHT OF WATER

Virginia, stones in pockets, laughs
with the river; bends halfway down
to meet its dark, brazen splash.

The family china is lonely: no solace
in spare rooms or morning's untidy sound.
Virginia, stones in pockets, laughs

at her own daring; wades deeper, past
the river's door; gently extends her hand
to meet its dark, brazen splash.

Ghosts in water: her children; Leonard's face,
lined with traces of the writer's wound.
Virginia, stones in pockets, laughs

at her own selfishness. She has not kept pace
with others. She craves river; will descend
to meet its dark, brazen splash.

She might at last be light; might unlace
her life, rich with river, deep and brown.
Virginia, stones in pockets, laughs
to meet its dark, brazen splash.

TWO THANKSGIVINGS

You, shrunken, vulnerable
in a hospital gown, reveal
newly defeated skin, as well
as doubts I haven't seen.
Recently, you seemed sturdy
as redwood bark; bruised,
translucent, your soul stuns me.

In a damask-draped Renaissance
villa by the Arno, we feasted on
a bowl of still life-worthy oranges;
reproductions of Michelangelo's
drawings; restored love, under glass.
Accustomed to our careful distance,
we couldn't tell what was authentic.

On this day of takeout turkey and
makeshift blessings, listless rain
fogs the window of your room.
You implore me to clean my plate;
adjust your pillow; fix the stars.

EQUILIBRIUM

If, inconsolable, we come weeping;
if, unquiet, we ask for muted sun;
if, spinning, we seek balance,
do not deny these contradictions.
In middle age, our perfect recall
of childhood's sting astonishes,
and so we wait for doors,
unyielding, to pry themselves
open; for playground bullies
to be kind; for mothers, fathers
to carry our eager faces,
already pressed and faded,
forever in their wallets,
plastic; peeling like the moon.

TOWARD POSITANO

Lemons. Fragrant with new starts.
We've come for them: posed photographs,
retouched; lustrous. Vines interwoven.
Memory's fictions.

We've come for this: the drive from Naples,
raucous *autostrada* turned suspicious
cliff; heart-in-mouth.
My easy cowardice, dear companion, is never far
from view. Damp with concentration, you tire
of our crumpled map; I fall silent.

If we drop precipitously, so be it.
We've been warned by bougainvillea
of love's curved limitations, tart;
final on the tongue.

MEMENTO MORI

Czeslaw Milosz died today.
We will observe silence.
We will write down life before we go.
We will invent words for time's
watery darkness; the blaze
of autumn's crenulated offerings.

We will revise the past in verse,
profuse in its ambrosial,
disinfecting properties.
Pale, naïve, we will not claim expertise,
nor speak of camps, gulags, cells:
hate's stench.

We will translate love, frequently
mistaken for its opposite;
we will catalog and file it for future
generations; lend them language of desire,
Janus-faced: wondrous skylight;
barbed caress.

We will fill out forms of solitude:
each confiscated heart,
trembling in exile,
will not learn the custom here;
will give itself away, all garish color,
for quick wine and lazy cigarettes.

We will invoke crocuses;
each lover's savior kiss;
a spurned voice, on the telephone,
whose pitch we cannot place;
crossed-out entries, long deceased,
in broken-spined address books.

If words were banned, consigned
to sewers bitter with soot, and tears;
if memory were spotty catechism;
if eyes were silenced,
stars would swear
Czeslaw Milosz died today.

GLASS

Such fear, its taste.
Ferrous oxide, semen, salt:
human ammunition, elements
of war, periodic table.
Symbols as remnants of science.
Mother's admonitions:
Tie your shoes. Button
up against the cold. It tightens
around you, this noose, night.
On being scared.
To each his own.
An aching vessel in the dark
of sight: your lair,
for better, for worse.

FOR MEDEA, WAKING

Sleep's black respite; blue, the rising day:
blurred fact of loss, fresh salt, in your eye,
on your tongue. Flung from the marriage
bed, unmoored, face newly ravaged
by revenge; yet, in cauterizing rage,
strange freedom, dimly lit. Bereft
by your own hand, you will not bathe
your sons again; never touch dear tendrils
of jet hair, violet-streaked. Wince
as you inhale desire's candied scent: once,
blended with Jason's pungent seed,
it bled you of youth. Wild orchids,
white beneath chariot wheels; history's archives
and your heart brim with endings: burnished,
endured. If men, coarse comrades
in gray wars, wield swords
which split fig-like flesh, and build
cities upon golden greed, or bile,
women too yield violent secrets:
quiet steel in bodily secretions
of water, fire, milk, birth; bitter paradox
for those who feed on them most
often. You, weary exile, forced to choose
between lover's blaze and mother's benign
kiss: recall, as you weep, supine
on crimson sheets, how the down on your arm
rose, sunlit fleece, with his stroke; harm
not yet done. Children could be soothed;
night's blade, sheathed; grief's stain, cleansed.

EPITAPH

Love, *sui generis*: your mother is gone.
Impermanence, a child's lament;
you are grown, yet cannot speak
of loss. We arrive at the cemetery's gate:
slender birch trees cannot shut the wind
out. Lives, connected, done up in brisk
sentences: "Wife, brother, daughter,
husband, beloved."Your tears
find my raincoat; I shiver, and offer
what love I can, poor substitute
for hers. We toss roses and dirt
onto the coffin embedded in Earth's
silent breach. Take my hand;
we'll reach home by dark.

AFTER ICARUS

No school for her today: there's nothing
left to learn. Pausing by church steps, she thinks
'I don't need this': ritual, prayer, a communion
dress stiff with starch and shyness.
In the square across town, laughter is a muted
bell; fruit vendors set out heavy mangoes, bananas;
women fry *churros*, and proudly display handmade
woven fabrics. She could spend last night's wages
on a linen cloth for her mother's kitchen table:
soon, it would show stains, like the rug, always wet
from her father's spilled *cervezas*; like her life,
or the undershirt her least favorite customer
wears. He smokes cigars and whimpers,
a baby, when he slams his pale, bloated body
into hers. Maybe next time, as he's doing it to her,
she'll think of the sea, custard cones, scent
of hibiscus on a breeze. Maybe salty wetness
on the inside of her thighs will replace tears
to wash away her shame. She's safe as long as
no man puts his lips on hers: that would make
her human; that would make her close her eyes.
Later, she'll burrow into the center of herself,
and wait for it to stop: the inevitable thump
of a rickety bed against a wall; his groan,
insistent train rumbling through mountains;
futile squawk of a chicken in dirt
below the window. Luck – radiant, silver,
a child's braided hair –
will swing back and forth,
pendulum with no resting place.

AS WITH EMMA BOVARY

Glittering rooms hold grave possibilities,
contradictions for those who pass
through: women, ravenous, wrists
encircled by seed pearl bracelets,
get caught on the arms of men resplendent
in peacock silks; women, eyes
of quicksilver, incite curious suitors
to covet corseted figures; men, duped by
candlelight, soon realize that hair, color
of wildfire, can never contain them; eyes,
unreliable, will not find them as they are.
Imperceptibly, dreams, heft of Limoges
cups, splinter. Invented lovers, rose-laden,
violet-lipped, may charge in on horseback;
bodies might be pleasure-singed. Such images,
sustenance for another day, pass
quickly through the heart.

For a long while, no faith in trees: knowing
all things green and lush will fall away.
Winter, merciless, withholding,

strips its branches, leaves them groaning
with the weight of lack, all frozen sway.
For a long while, no faith in trees: knowing

time will snap, with frost's first closing
in on night's blank roof, blackened reverie.
Winter, merciless, withholding,

steels itself against young emotion, scorning
spring, soothsayer of a verdant day.
For a long while, no faith in trees: knowing

how a lover's rhyme lingers on skin; longing
for each bloom, exuberant with melody.
Winter, merciless, withholding,

plants the moon in bas-relief, taunting
us with icy heat, voluptuous fantasy.
For a long while, no faith in trees: knowing
winter, merciless, withholding.

WINGING IT

Birds, their day of reckoning;
reconciled to a ripped-up sky,
they circumvent shredded clouds
which once gleamed with
possibility. Havens, silver-lined,
gone. The birds, that day –
migration to farthest shores.
Life will be better, a cozy homily
cross-stitched on pillows
small enough for bird-sized heads.

Days, stored away behind crumbling
clouds, color of archival paper.
Nothing keeps.
Birds, of course, know this.

HIGH DIVE

Now, he wouldn't take
the risk of injury
to the head,
or to the spinal cord,
already severed, neatly,
in night *mers*.
Back then, his brain

grew homesick
when not fluid-encased;
sought artificial seas
every chance it got.
And so he plunged his body,
brave with love,
into chlorinated pools.

His eyes stung
from these excursions;
from the beauty
he'd seen more than once:
mirage, or mermaid,
lounging by each pool.
She smelled of freesia,

and summer, unending.
She wasn't meant
to be attained, just
admired from the distance
of each diving board
on which he stood,
hope pooling at his feet.

RIVER, MEMORIZED
(for J.S.)

I.

Back then, I hadn't learned their names:
Tigris, Yangtze, Rhine, Euphrates,
Vistula, Amazon, Danube, Guadalquivir.
Back then, I didn't know the world;
you, wise, were the world. I was almost six,
cocooned in summer happiness:
our New Jersey cottage, humble shingles
amid grand homes, year-round families;
collapsed marshmallows, molten clouds;
yellow pajamas, crisp sun, on the clothesline;
walks to town, vanilla cones, small arm linked
with strong one; ducks, sweet guests, roaming
our porch after the Ramapo swelled
and crept across the road.

II.

That morning, wanting to be brave for you, and
old, I marched, resolute, chubby in a plaid
two-piece bathing suit, clutching my plastic
dolphin tube, down slippery-sharp dock
steps; I pierced mossy, mud-lined water:
gooey thrill, smooth, icy roller coaster;
no warning, just tube's whoosh, wounded air;
down, down, down, green to brown to black:
empty, endless water, no horizon line;
swallowing, shouting, reaching, holding on

to ledge, fickle rock, your faraway face. Strong,
late, you yanked me up, out of this Acheron: sudden
knowledge, rough baptism. Choking on river, tears, dry
reassurances, I couldn't trust you. Once, you were the world.

III.
Empty trust, that morning almost ten years later:
floodwater rushed in, above, below, heart, throat;
no warning, just Monday, level, slow;
no wise note of leaving, no swallow, shout,
reach; no holding on to my close
face, shy semblance of your blue-eyed smile.
I didn't know death had a name. Lost, you were the world.

IV.
I want to be brave, and old;
I've almost learned the world.
I still wear two-piece bathing suits;
ice cream in August slakes
my fever. I'm coming up on your age,
then: I hold on when December's
dark river erodes one more year.
I've touched the Tiber and Seine;
the Thames, many others; perhaps one
day, I'll know the Nile. I quietly recite
these names, and yours, each time
a man reaches for me and leads
my willing body down slippery-sharp steps
into exotic, spiraling water.

Desire and Memory

INSOMNIA

Darkness, the focus on desire: does it propel the heart,
or keep it under house arrest? Best not to ask.
Moon, reckless, says "It's you I want." *I want.*
The stomach's slender appetite; fire, in the groin:
I grow fond of these sensations, hidden;
confessed, in schoolgirl whispers, to pink hydrangeas;
rain, empathetic; pigeons in the park.
I fool my recent lovers: each quick
intake of breath, sly moan, is meant for you, not them.
I get no younger; still, perhaps there's time
to solve Fermat's Last Theorem, or join
the debate on black holes. I'll sing arias; paint;
build a studio in Taos. Resume my life in noon's brilliant
light. Your name – night's poem – will wake me.

ORNITHOLOGY

You, slanting inside me: cormorant,
sudden dark, glossed with lust.
Hungry for what I cannot be:
lost youth, seized.

Predators, we skim the sea, gold-stained;
satiety, our feathered prospect,
held aloft.

Arc in stolen sky above me, close;
pierce me with your need
for a resting place.

Your eyes – gold-rimmed,
flecked with years, hope's debris –
scratch my breast,
cool perch beneath your parched beak.

Use untrimmed talons, greedy skin;
revere all instincts, base.
Devour what we do not grasp: daylight.

With steel-cut wings, triangular,
tether me to mournful cries;
to this brief morning.

Spent, we will forage for noon
on the cusp of the sun.

BETRAYAL

Caught mid-dream, in lust's dense
forest, rapier-branched: restless,
repeated plight. Your sprawled,
spilled form wrestles
with this wrinkled void called bed,
or sleep; the body's accelerated
rhythms inconsolable now.
Hands, docile by day, clench
under moonlight's interrogatory
gaze. Alert to every shift in mood,
desire's leash drags you along
its nocturnal road; your steps,
recalcitrant, will cause regret
come morning.

WITH THANKS TO MAGRITTE AND DUCHAMP

Kiss me like you mean it —
brazen kiss of a comet
auditioning, with conviction,
for its niche in a seen-it-all *ciel*;
for its spot
on your mantel,
beside your pipe dreams;
the Surrealist volumes,
vials of truth serum,
lying in wait
for this type of occasion.
Strip off the bridal
cloth which veils us;
relinquish bachelor-ed modesty.

PERMISSION

(after James Merrill)

I do not trust myself not to dial your number.
I have decided to write this poem instead.

A friend, wise in love, shared plain advice:
"Do not go to the hardware store if you want

to buy apples." The end, in our beginning:
you confided you were damaged; far from wise

in love's affairs. "Do not invest the time,"
you said. "Do not think you can improve me."

What you did then, what you did, was take my face
in your hands. You asked permission for a kiss,

as if I were a girl in a novel by Trollope or Austen.
I should have listened to wisdom. Instead,

I leaned in for one kiss. One: misleading number.

FORGIVE ME IF NONE OF THIS IS TRUE
(for R.S.)

From a nautilus shell, silver-pink, jagged,
vapor leaks, obscuring the sun's ancient rituals.
An infant, resilient chimera, rises: cerulean eyes, chilled fire.
Child of Zeus and Demeter, she has one foot
in Hades, the other in spring and summer.
Verdant, languorous, she is thorns and opals
woven together in a lustrous shawl.
She'll wear it easily; it will be shelter, shield, invitation.

What I'd like to clasp
eludes me,
sleeping reminder:
your fingers, orange-scented,
scattering jeweled fragments
on the ornate tray atop your dressing table.

The yard is different; trees, the same.
The attic is emptied out;
the kitchen is yellowed linoleum;
the living room is tired sheets over broken chairs.

You could be moving in or evacuating.

I thought I'd gotten away.

You are loose-skinned, beseeching, smaller;
I am old, and don't need you as much.
You feed off my arm, and ask why I never call.

I tell you I don't know the number here;
I had it in kindergarten, it was pinned to my mitten.
Now it's a torn scrap holding a book in its place.

I bathe you, and straighten up;
truth, caught in the net of your eel-gray eyes,
eludes me.

Empires come and go.

Persephone was born of a merciless sea;
she crashed, luxuriously, into its depths,
up, out again.
This fluid mother,
shrewd assessor of her mettle,
forced life into her, then tossed her,

gasping, onto sharp, white rocks,
knowing that she'd stand on brittle legs,
and stumble toward brightness.

I'd so like another chance to get this right:
if my outstretched palms
could match yours, we'd end the dream now.

You, presiding over this velvet, hallucinatory room,
would recede as I stir awake.

Once, your warm proximity
made me swoon with a daughter's pleasure.
This was Eden: pre-Father, pre-Adam;

no encroaching member of the other sex,
the thickly muscled shoulder.

Not yet dark waves; not new drowning,
nor exquisite shudder.

PALIMPSEST

Recline with me; I will explain,
in wordless paragraphs,
a foreign alphabet,
how we came to be here.
Assist me in the undoing of hooks
and eyes. Peel back night's
onionskin: this life, scratched-out,
begun again. Uncap, as an offering,
your fountain pen; dip it lightly in ink
impenetrable as a 3 a.m. sky.
You will draw Chinese characters:
unrecognizable, perhaps,
yet your pen will move rapidly
over my parchment.

GRATITUDE

When we are done, I'll thank you for this night.
We're returning home from dinner out,
a corny tourist trap in Little Italy,
candles in emptied Chianti bottles. Sated, silly
with watered-down *vino*, we weave,
laughing, along Soho streets; our talk, nonsense.
The sheen of sex clings to us: bliss, its blush,
all pink-tinged promise. On Wooster,
an elderly couple walks past us, a memory:
what it was to live
for a lover's touch; the burn, the wet, the sigh.
When the wine wears off, some word,
a gesture of mine, will annoy you.
You'll forget this night, our intoxication.

FORTUNE

Remembering past generosity,
he marvels at her body's subtle turning;
thinks back on misplaced nights
when, porous, warm, she would take him in.
He was a refugee from bone-cold rain.
She was happy to oblige his plea for heat,
or asylum from the mind's black
mutterings. They seemed, to him, to come
in waves on nights misplaced.
Thinking back, he wonders if her body's
subtle turning toward his own,
his pulsing counterparts –
penis, heart – augured kindness,
or merely resignation.

SITTING OUT THE SEASON

As a boy, you loved the sport —
crack of bat on ball; the sense that sky
was possible. Life, tall, right

before you: jade spires of grass licking
your ankles in spring, lazy
joy; sighting home, stealing time.

As a young man in the game,
you caught a girl, her power in a dress
slight as tissue paper, fanned across

cream thighs. Hint of goddess, glimpse
of sky: famished innocence, lust;
anticipation of the possible.

Immortal then, you strode gray fields —
crack of mortar shell above your shoulder;
darkened thrill of grown-up games,

preferred private wars. Ball of fire
in your chest, comet in the sky: the future,
safe from twisted limbs in trenches.

By middle age, hesitant velocity,
thick, unfamiliar; a reticent survivor, gloveless
dinner table battles; all curve, no fly.

In death, you grip a blood-stitched ball,
compact sphere of hope. Aloof,
the shining grass;

the sky will not be pierced.

SUMMER OF LOVE

I was too old, just born, for barefoot, daisy-in-the-hair abandon.
I was too young to understand that free love is an oxymoron.
I was too straight for mind-altering, encapsulated substances.
I would have liked to change the world by sitting on warm grass,
and chanting, or waving ink-stained fingers, silent sign of peace.
The world is late for change. Each word alters my mind.
The other drug is you: you never have come free.
So I pluck petals from new daisies, innocent bystanders:
I ask if you love me; love me not. The day depends on it.
You are my LSD, altering perceptions. I expand;
dance on the head of a pin. No sensible dose
of you: as such, residual damage to my nervous system.

Startled by something green, sunlit,
I throw back my head; laugh; lie down in your field.

GARDEN

If I could identify plants by their Latin names,
I would get down on my hands and knees,
try to soothe the dirt; coax life from it.
If I could be your Eve — silly temptress, hormones raging —
I would get down on my hands and knees,
take you, with love, impatiently (*impatiens*: herb
with irregular flowers, also known as *jewelweed*.)
I would be purple, flame, magenta for you: un-shy colors.
Gladiolus. Glad to see you. I am not fluent in flowers;
I pronounce words which sound like the heart,
root of beauty: blood-red root. *Coeur. Corazón.*
Corazón sangrante. Cuore. Courage, my love, my heart.
You grow in this poem; are rooted in the flower's bed.
You emerge from ground, grisaille by night.

You burgeon here: your boyhood strongbox of ghosts
and dreams is buried in this patient soil. I would not strike
the dirt, or reveal the heart before its blooming.
You grow sons, a daughter; you have your own seed.
You do not need my scattered offering,
but keep it in your pocket: faith, to soothe your seasons.
You grow sons, a daughter.
Rain and wind will intrude as you tell them of spring,
greener than the sum of its seeds. As you are.
As you will change with what is given.
I pronounce you rare.
I plant shy words which sound like spring.
I identify you by your Latin name: eternal syllables,
arising from soil.

THREAD

Dark unspooling, as we fasten ourselves
to a point larger than night.
Flash of filament:
proof that we begin exactly here.
Later, we will pattern
our own ending,
but in this workroom
we are draped in celestial fabric;
we are rounded, smooth, extravagant.
Love cannot rupture.
Time, paid by the hour,
labors with its thimble.
Endearments glint;
catch on the bedpost.

X-RAY VISION
(for S.D.L.)

Revealed in a colorless cubicle, I regress,
under ultra-violet light, to the primitive place
where frozen metal meets flesh and rib;
inconvenient tears thaw chin
and clavicle; latex-sheathed fingers,
incurious, stroke my wistful spaces.

Remember how, as kids, we looked
forward to Halloween?
You, scary skeleton, raced ahead
of me in darkness. I was a good witch,
blue-silver, shimmery: tinfoil wand
in one hand; in the other,
your agitated heart,
released from its white-boned cage.

WHAT THE EYE NO LONGER SEES WITH LOVE

An orphaned house, dank, creased:
frowning shutters hang in cracked
folds around its blank, unlifted face;
late day wind broods, pretend-fierce.
Bitter orange peel and piles of eggshells
litter a battered breakfast table, exiled
to empty conversation with a rusted garden faucet.
With no beloved to reflect it, a face is just a face.

On splintered stairs we kissed, ravenous;
our grasping hands cast
glittering nets over hazardous places.
Without the sun, a face is just a shadowed face.

Untouched, the tear-encrusted cup;
unlatched, the cupboard where bent stars are kept.

VISITATION RIGHTS

Come sit beside me on this bench:
notice how the red-haired boy
hoards fistfuls of his mother's skirt
as if his fate depends on it.

The park twirls summer deftly,
pledging not to tire of her.
Once, you dipped me in a slow lake:
uncoiled, I swam, shaded by desire.

When we first rested here, you spoke
in promises: fidelity, and fire.
Greedily, you took my hand, the knot
of your fingers silken, unyielding.

Regardless of what you declared,
regardless of what I hold sacred,
a slippery sun will fall from grass
as we part for good.

THAW

First, a loosening; soon, winter's
plaintive wail evaporates.

Distant, your icy whisper;
its shards no longer penetrate.

Tulip bulbs I'd planted beneath
my solstice skin fill me;

I breathe again. Sky-scented,
verdant, I crave languor,

as when I was love-new,
wet; bright-petalled, for you.

Branches, rugged, embrace
me: seductive in roseate light,

their ardor dims as day
and I come to a moist parting.

GHOST

So changed you are, walking up the street.
I'm waiting for you in front of a dive coffee shop.
Shock: it isn't just the gone-gray hair, pulled back
into a rocker's ponytail, a look that did not suit
you, even in youth. The black ringlets, a mother's
pride, have disappeared; your face, gaunt
with disappointment, shakes me to the core.
You always said I was optimist enough for both of us.
I loved you just as surely as gravity:
was pulled, deeper by the day, into your center.
We thought we'd hold together, unblinking, despite
passion's wavering denial of its whereabouts.
I forget the *why* of things.
You've become a hologram; I can't ask you.

BALANCING
(for J.S.)

There was one nearly perfect day,
prelude to your death,

when light and prayer hung low
in gleaming, hopeful air.

I was an out-of-breath young girl,
all flying legs and hair,

seeming to swirl on a pearly rink
engraved with dreaming circles.

You, mournful father outside my arms,
never felt my weightless longing.

There was such white meaning
in this dance: I pliéd, proud,

a nascent swan who'd melt
your lonely marriage pond,

and spin with you.
You knelt to lace my loosened skate,

poorly cross-stitched scar.
Regret's blade left welts upon the ice.

Afternoon bled into dusk.

Afraid your face will fade,
certain that it will,

I wish that I could warm my hands
and sit with you awhile.

PREPARING FOR TAKEOFF

Whenever I had an attack of nerves,
I would cut crusts off plum jam sandwiches;
feed them to swallows on the boardwalk near my yellow house.
These birds could digest fear, lust; yet achieve velocity.
I, inspired, would flap my arms; hope for momentum.
Perched on the roof, I could rush past
other planets, substitutes for home.

Often, strapped into the backseat of a taxi,
I would hold on for dear life; squeeze my eyes shut;
convince myself that the driver, fearless, should fly that fast.
His impulse: to get on with it.
Often, as we kissed in the backseat of a taxi,
you would unbutton my coat and sweater; release the straps;
put your lips where they could find momentum.

Whenever you were cajoling; fearless;
impatient with the stoplights,
I could convince you, and myself, to wait.
All those signals, pop art lollipops, seduction for the mouth:
they didn't halt our impulse
to risk flight; reconsider; finally succumb.
Hungry for home, we would rush past timid planets.

PAS DE DEUX

Wordless sighting, windblown street:
you (elegant; white-caned; gray-jacketed)
have an air of proper belonging.
I'm moved by your grasp of what goes forward.

Years back, you stared into a forgiving mirror,
and admired what you saw: frank temptress,
laughter, store-bought gardenia behind the ear.
You imagined moon, pleasure, scented air;
ripe pears in the morning, tequila after supper.
You wanted a certain man to knock the floor out
from under you with his mouth and fingertips.

Things change. There is no mirror.
You'd like to pause, but this swirling corner
has other plans. Your voice brims
with time and formality; I take your arm
before others move between us, drawn
by shifting light.

IN THE DARKROOM

This welcome, silent second chance
to change the past, and filter out black spots.
An exposed heart dodges
all that's negative, or scratched.

Liquid scents of leaving, pungent,
strip beds of regret;
a kiss, blank, is not lost on wintry sheets
salt-blurred, and wet.

Flick of the magician's wrist:
perspectives, faded; forlorn lovers
floating into view.
Strange light is fixed; vows, renewed.

Shadowed by a swollen clock,
memory, sly witness, cloaks
and burns its sins.
Truth emerges, blushing; falsely positive.

FREEZING THE WORLD
(for L.G.)

The eyes photograph each tiny world,
tundra, desert, flower field
floating above the fray
of hoarse humanity.

Love refutes each graveyard:
chiffon cage, a lottery won;
detergent snow stuck to eyes,
mistaken for permanent fire.

Go on, wrap the solar system
in anodyne fabric;
in mother's joyful swoons,
and lover's hushed denial.

Unspeak the teardrop
of mortality,
mesh cage of limits.

ENTRANCE

Like a jittery butterfly,
you arrived far too early,
sliding, in one tender,
essential breath,
down the steps of my womb.
A nurse who'd taken a vow
of tact appraised you
under bleached hospital light.
Swaddled in afterbirth and faint
violin sounds of winter,
you bowed, shyly,
with the night.

CUTTING OUT HOUSES
(for R. S.)

In after-school winter dark, intent on our handiwork,
we'd cut perfect shapes from red construction paper:
houses, fences, parents, children, flowers.
Other colors, too; red remained your favorite.
You hummed a plangent tune.
When vibrant, you were mine.

Saturday nights, out with Dad, you wore brocade and furs.
Did I mention that I've kept your sewing scissors?
We'd cut and paste the future, virginal with hope.
I revered you; was frightened of your displeasure.
That time I broke the table leg; that time you wouldn't answer.
I've done penance for my childish ways.

Did I mention that I have your walk?
You were giving, but with strings.
What you taught: grieving doesn't stop.
How carefully we'd cut the future into shapes
of our own making: green, orange, blue, yellow, mostly red.
I wonder if you'd recognize this life, its uneven edges.

I reminisce: you, red-haired beacon in winter's jarring dark,
setting our dinner table.
Careful preparation; what a girl should know.
I wear your amethysts, golden string of past decades,
dear keepsakes in a box:
cool scissors, and a cut-out heart.

CAST-IRON

The pan was black with repeated use and poverty.
Your grandmother's sight was poor,
her fingers heavy with arthritis and sacrifice.
She seasoned the pan with salt, oil and cayenne.
She sang hymns which referenced promised lands,
life's valleys, and the Lord, provider of plenty.
When there was next to nothing left,
she fried up catfish, or chicken:
dipped it, naked, gleaming, into flour before
tossing it, with potato and onion,
into the pan.

Sometimes, your grandmother hummed along
to the radio, or to the moonshine sounds
within her soul. Smells of home, food
and smoke, rose in bluesy vapors;
climbed beyond the kitchen, settling
into the sitting room's cabbage rose-patterned
wallpaper. After supper, your grandmother
wiped the pan not-quite-clean; left
its seasonings intact. Sometimes,
she let you hum along,
even though you couldn't carry a tune.

CULPABILITY

The rain, vertical metronome,
has much in common
with this refrain: "*Why, love, why?*"
Confess everything in great detail.
What you wore, what you consumed
on the night in question.
What the air smelled of, jasmine
or tar. Who followed whom.
An urgent need to know;
a breakdown in the system.
Sad, but a relief, to hear rain
tapping out the sound of goodbye
in Morse code
against the misted-over window.

BLUE MATTRESS

It rests on discarded snow.
Sleep's raft, torn sea, beached satin whale.
The heart has sprung dry leaks by now.

Entrails, coiled, exposed to shallow
passersby. Salt-stained love, chill tale.
It rests on discarded snow.

In youth, it shone. Bridal gown
tossed there, honeymoon-night gale.
The heart has sprung dry leaks by now.

Bodies crested. Doubt was drowned
in firm, tufted waves. Passion, pale.
It rests on discarded snow.

Children sailed tall tears on it, found
solace when the cradle failed.
The heart has sprung dry leaks by now.

Windblown, winter's marriage vow.
Forlorn bed, iced-over grail.
It rests on discarded snow.
The heart has sprung dry leaks by now.

UNLIKE RAPUNZEL

Every night and then
with morning, she checked
the glass for her sworn
reflection: proof that she
was not obsolete.
Routine, lazy jailer, dictated
that she let down
her hair, pinned by night,
and tucked into sleep.
Hair, more gray than brown,
wrong for its fashion,
stretched below her waist;
almost touched the floor
of her princeless tower.

SUNDAY

Again, the tousled dream of you;
I must change, or burn, the bed linen:
it kept us company on the *rapido* from Milan
to Rome, but I can no longer afford
such luxury. Awake, aware of compression:
you, crowding last night's wine,
what kind of computer to buy; leaves,
their colors; irregular French verbs.
Splayed newspapers offer millions of words;
I choose your name, boldfaced,
and place my fingers on this Braille: blind
notion that you equal happiness.
I must purge closets for charity;
I must cook your favorite meal, and preserve it;
I must propitiate gods in selfish ways;
I must set clocks back, ahead;
I must outwit the concept
of your incendiary skin
and evade the answering machine's
bloodshot wink, which might be you
finding someone else
or failing at sleep without me.

TRISTESSE

Today, a different blue;
it defies description.
Not robin's egg, not royal;
not navy, aqua, ocean.

The years swim slowly
in our brain to form an epic poem;
not epic like *The Illiad* or *The Odyssey*,
but sprawling nonetheless.

The spoken and the speechless:
pre-dawn waves undulate;
stake their claim
to our imagination.

Years hold us down, immune
to cries for mercy.
A peaceful dread today:
at last, a different blue.

REFUSAL

Eventually, old age's
camphor smell will seep

from my skin, startling
my complacent bones.

I will then decline
invitations to the dance;

will scrape mascara
from my eyes;

remove silk stockings
and gold shoes;

inform my beaux
that I no longer have

the stamina for love.

I wish to sleep in peace.

TIDES

Under striped awning sky, children fill
tiny pails with sand: cities, built as shovels click
against shells hidden in dirt; new civilizations,
forged in the undertow. I watch out for these children;
mothers, reclining, can't keep them afloat. Absent,
weekday fathers: cries of "Daddy, come look at me"

flail about. Once, swallowed by dreams
I saw day, buoyant, sink into sundown;
my face and shoulders shone, shame's
heat, as I waited for Father to find
me beautiful. I poured sand into pails, stand-ins for
his eyes, and planned new infrastructures of the heart.

Drunk on summer solitude, children slip,
with their castles, into an ocean's outstretched arms.

NANTUCKET MORNING

I escape from this house, its sharp edges
hidden by dawn's white gauze:
a furtive leaning into the sea.
Memory's horizon line snakes
across the drowsy beach;
my sunburned heart
conjures you, golden, as you were
when, lazy with desire,
you would swim into me. As I run,
neighboring houses – salt-pocked,
harmless – fall away, obscured
by weeds and dunes. The wind,
brash accomplice, erases my footprints,
if only to prove a point.

DAY OF ATONEMENT

In the moments left
before light moves on
I say I'm sorry.
While speech, dear, remains free
I say I love you.
As I fumble with the greeting
for an ending,
I say I feel you
in each season's turning;
I hear you
when night's cello plays, low;
as rain takes the edge off stones.
Such humble gestures will be lost
if time has its way.

Afterword by the Author

This book has gestated for years: I wrote the poems included in this volume between 2001 and 2014.

All writers are indebted to their readers; to poets, they are truly invaluable.

My heartfelt thanks to you for investing time, money and thought in this collection.

Ilene Starger

About the Author

Ilene Starger is a New York-born poet and writer. Her work has been published in *Bayou, Oyez Review, Georgetown Review, Tributaries, Folio, Oberon, Paper Street, Second Wind, Tar Wolf Review, Erato, Grasslimb, Manzanita, Poesia, Ibbetson Street, Iodine, Phoenix, The New Renaissance, The Same*, and online in the *Tupelo Press Poetry Project, The Istanbul Literary Review and Levure Littéraire*. She received Honorable Mention citations for the 2004 Ann Stanford Poetry Prize sponsored by the *Southern California Anthology*, and for the 2005 *New Millennium Writings* Competition; she was a finalist for the 2005 Ann Stanford Poetry Prize. She received Honorable Mention citations for the 2006 Oliver Browning Poetry Competition sponsored by *Poesia* and Indian Bay Press, and for the 2007 Poetry Competition sponsored by Writecorner Press. Finishing Line Press published her chapbook *Lethe, Postponed* in 2008. She is the co-creator of *Elusive Things*, a classical song cycle composed by Eric Shimelonis based on ten of her poems. *Elusive Things*, sung by F. Murray Abraham, with music played by the musicians of Voice of the City Ensemble, had its premiere at Weill Recital Hall at Carnegie Hall on January 15, 2010. She is currently at work on various writing projects.

Made in United States
North Haven, CT
27 January 2025

65037986R00086